THE
WORLD
IS YOUR
OYSTER

summersdale

THE WORLD IS YOUR OYSTER

Copyright © Summersdale Publishers Ltd, 2015

Summersdale Publishers Ltd
46 West Street
Chichester
West Sussex
PO19 1RP
UK

www.summersdale.com

Printed and bound in the Czech Republic

ISBN: 978-1-84953-689-9

Substantial discounts on bulk quantities of Summersdale books are available to corporations, professional associations and other organisations. For details contact Nicky Douglas by telephone: +44 (0) 1243 756902, fax: +44 (0) 1243 786300 or email: nicky@summersdale.com.

TO.....................................

FROM.................................

DREAMS DO COME TRUE,
IF WE ONLY WISH
HARD ENOUGH.

J. M. Barrie

ONCE YOU REPLACE
NEGATIVE THOUGHTS
WITH POSITIVE ONES,
YOU'LL START HAVING
POSITIVE RESULTS.

Willie Nelson

TODAY IS A
BLANK PAGE —
WHAT ARE YOU
GOING TO WRITE
ON IT?

YOU HAVE TO BE STRONG
AND COURAGEOUS AND
KNOW THAT YOU CAN DO
ANYTHING YOU PUT
YOUR MIND TO.

Leah LaBelle

WHEN YOU COME TO
A ROADBLOCK, TAKE
A DETOUR.

Mary Kay Ash

LIFE IS SWEET –
TAKE A BIG BITE!

TO SUCCEED, YOU NEED TO
FIND SOMETHING TO HOLD
ON TO, SOMETHING TO
MOTIVATE YOU, SOMETHING
TO INSPIRE YOU.

Tony Dorsett

IN ORDER TO CARRY A
POSITIVE ACTION, WE
MUST DEVELOP HERE A
POSITIVE VISION.

Dalai Lama

IT'S TIME TO
SHOW THE WORLD
WHAT YOU'RE
MADE OF!

I BELIEVE IN WRITING YOUR OWN STORY.

Charlotte Eriksson

PROGRESS IS A NICE
WORD. BUT CHANGE IS
ITS MOTIVATOR.

Robert F. Kennedy

YOU'RE NEVER LOST
— YOU'RE JUST
DISCOVERING
NEW PLACES

OPTIMISTS MOVE
THROUGH LIFE WITH
A HAPPY EXTERIOR.
WHAT HAPPENS ON THE
INSIDE SHOWS UP ON
THE OUTSIDE.

Marilyn Suttle

ALL GREAT ACHIEVEMENTS REQUIRE TIME.

Maya Angelou

STAND OUT FROM THE CROWD – MAKE AN IMPRESSION!

WE BECOME HAPPIER,
MUCH HAPPIER, WHEN
WE REALISE LIFE IS AN
OPPORTUNITY RATHER
THAN AN OBLIGATION.

Mary Augustine

TRUST IN DREAMS,
FOR IN THEM IS HIDDEN
THE GATE TO ETERNITY.

Kahlil Gibran

LOOK FOR
THE FLOWERS
THAT GROW UP
THROUGH THE
CRACKS

PESSIMISM LEADS TO WEAKNESS, OPTIMISM TO POWER.

William James

TO SUCCEED IN
LIFE, YOU NEED TWO
THINGS: IGNORANCE
AND CONFIDENCE.

Mark Twain

DON'T SHRINK
FROM A
CHALLENGE —
EMBRACE IT!

THE MOST EFFECTIVE WAY TO DO IT IS TO DO IT.

Amelia Earhart

THE STARTING POINT OF ALL ACHIEVEMENT IS DESIRE.

Napoleon Hill

LET NOTHING
HOLD YOU BACK!

THE BACKBONE OF
SUCCESS IS... HARD
WORK, DETERMINATION,
GOOD PLANNING AND
PERSEVERANCE.

Mia Hamm

LIFE ISN'T A MATTER
OF MILESTONES, BUT
OF MOMENTS.

Rose Kennedy

MAKE YOUR OWN
SUNSHINE

A SUCCESSFUL MAN IS
ONE WHO CAN LAY A
FIRM FOUNDATION WITH
THE BRICKS OTHERS
HAVE THROWN AT HIM.

David Brinkley

IT'S WHERE WE GO, AND
WHAT WE DO WHEN WE
GET THERE, THAT TELLS
US WHO WE ARE.

Joyce Carol Oates

LIFE IS NOT
A DRESS
REHEARSAL —
ENJOY YOUR
TIME IN THE
LIMELIGHT!

I DON'T MEASURE A
MAN'S SUCCESS BY HOW
HIGH HE CLIMBS BUT
HOW HIGH HE BOUNCES
WHEN HE HITS BOTTOM.

George S. Patton

POSITIVE ANYTHING
IS BETTER THAN
NEGATIVE NOTHING.

Elbert Hubbard

LIVE FOR TODAY
AND FORGET
THE PAST

THE ROUGHEST ROADS OFTEN LEAD TO THE TOP.

Christina Aguilera

WE FALL FORWARD
TO SUCCEED.

Mary Kay Ash

YOUR LIFE IS A
WORK OF ART —
BE PROUD TO
DISPLAY IT

FORMAL EDUCATION WILL
MAKE YOU A LIVING;
SELF-EDUCATION WILL
MAKE YOU A FORTUNE.

Jim Rohn

NO ATTAINMENT IS
BEYOND HIS REACH WHO
EQUIPS HIMSELF WITH
PATIENCE TO ACHIEVE IT.

Jean de La Bruyère

START SOMETHING
NEW TODAY,
HOWEVER SMALL

SUCCESS COMES FROM
KNOWING THAT YOU DID
YOUR BEST TO BECOME
THE BEST THAT YOU ARE
CAPABLE OF BECOMING.

John Wooden

ONLY THOSE WHO DARE
TO FAIL GREATLY CAN
EVER ACHIEVE GREATLY.

Robert F. Kennedy

GO OUT THERE
AND GRAB LIFE!

TO BECOME SUCCESSFUL,
ONE MUST PUT
THEMSELVES IN THE
PATHS OF GIANTS!

Lillian Cauldwell

LIVE LIFE TO THE
FULLEST, AND FOCUS
ON THE POSITIVE.

Matt Cameron

MAKE FRIENDS
WITH NEW
PEOPLE TODAY!

MUSCLES ACHING TO WORK, MINDS ACHING TO CREATE — THIS IS MAN.

John Steinbeck

EVERY GREAT DREAM
BEGINS WITH A DREAMER.

Harriet Tubman

SHINE LIKE
A STAR

FRUSTRATION, ALTHOUGH
QUITE PAINFUL AT
TIMES, IS A VERY
POSITIVE AND ESSENTIAL
PART OF SUCCESS.

Bo Bennett

IT IS NOT IN THE STARS
TO HOLD OUR DESTINY
BUT IN OURSELVES.

William Shakespeare

LIFE IS NOT
ABOUT WINNING
OR LOSING —
IT'S ABOUT
TAKING PART

SUCCESS IS A SCIENCE;
IF YOU HAVE THE
CONDITIONS, YOU GET
THE RESULT.

Oscar Wilde

GET ACTION. SEIZE THE
MOMENT. MAN WAS
NEVER INTENDED TO
BECOME AN OYSTER.

Theodore Roosevelt

TODAY IS THE
FIRST DAY OF
THE REST OF
YOUR LIFE

THE FUTURE BELONGS
TO THOSE WHO BELIEVE
IN THE BEAUTY OF
THEIR DREAMS.

Eleanor Roosevelt

EACH MAN IN HIS WAY
IS A TREASURE.

Robert Falcon Scott

HAVE THE
COURAGE
OF YOUR
CONVICTIONS

THAT WHICH DOES NOT KILL US MAKES US STRONGER.

Friedrich Nietzsche

SUCCESS ISN'T A
RESULT OF SPONTANEOUS
COMBUSTION. YOU MUST
SET YOURSELF ON FIRE.

Arnold H. Glasow

BELIEVE IN
YOURSELF ~ YOU
ARE AMAZING!

THE BRAVE MAN IS NOT
HE WHO DOES NOT FEEL
AFRAID, BUT HE WHO
CONQUERS THAT FEAR.

Nelson Mandela

THERE IS NO REASON
TO NOT FOLLOW YOUR
HEART... STAY HUNGRY.
STAY FOOLISH.

Steve Jobs

YOU ARE THE HERO OF YOUR STORY

MANKIND AT ITS MOST
DESPERATE IS OFTEN
AT ITS BEST.

Bob Geldof

WE ARE ALL IN THE
GUTTER, BUT SOME OF
US ARE LOOKING AT
THE STARS.

Oscar Wilde

WHAT ARE YOU WAITING FOR? TAKE ACTION!

ONCE WE ACCEPT
OUR LIMITS, WE GO
BEYOND THEM.

Albert Einstein

HE WAS A BOLD MAN
THAT FIRST ATE
AN OYSTER.

Jonathan Swift

ENJOY THE
JOURNEY OF
LIFE WITH ALL
ITS TWISTS AND
TURNS

THE FINEST STEEL HAS TO GO THROUGH THE HOTTEST FIRE.

Anonymous

IT ALWAYS SEEMS
IMPOSSIBLE UNTIL
IT'S DONE.

Nelson Mandela

DON'T WAIT FOR
GOOD THINGS TO
HAPPEN — GO OUT
AND GET THEM!

SUCCESS ISN'T
MEASURED BY MONEY OR
POWER OR SOCIAL RANK.
SUCCESS IS MEASURED
BY YOUR DISCIPLINE AND
INNER PEACE.

Mike Ditka

LIVE AS IF YOU WERE
TO DIE TOMORROW.
LEARN AS IF YOU WERE
TO LIVE FOR EVER.

Mahatma Gandhi

WISH UPON A
STAR, THEN
MAKE IT COME
TRUE!

HE WHO HAS A WHY
TO LIVE CAN BEAR
ALMOST ANY HOW.

Friedrich Nietzsche

ONE DOES NOT DISCOVER
NEW LANDS WITHOUT
CONSENTING TO LOSE
SIGHT OF THE SHORE
FOR A VERY LONG TIME.

André Gide

REPLACE THE WORD 'CHALLENGE' WITH 'OPPORTUNITY'

I HAVE NOT FAILED.
I'VE JUST FOUND
10,000 WAYS THAT
WON'T WORK.

Thomas Edison

YOU HAVE BRAINS IN YOUR
HEAD. YOU HAVE FEET
IN YOUR SHOES. YOU CAN
STEER YOURSELF ANY
DIRECTION YOU CHOOSE.

Dr Seuss

CHALLENGE
CONVENTION

COMMITMENT LEADS TO
ACTION. ACTION BRINGS
YOUR DREAM CLOSER.

Marcia Wieder

IT IS NEVER TOO
LATE TO BE WHAT YOU
MIGHT HAVE BEEN.

George Eliot

TAKE SOMETHING
POSITIVE FROM
EVERY SITUATION

DO WHAT YOU CAN,
WITH WHAT YOU HAVE,
WHERE YOU ARE.

Theodore Roosevelt

THIS LIFE IS WHAT YOU MAKE IT.

Marilyn Monroe

WRITE A BOOK, CREATE ART — CHANGE THE WORLD

COURAGE ISN'T HAVING
THE STRENGTH TO GO
ON — IT IS GOING ON
WHEN YOU DON'T HAVE
STRENGTH.

Napoleon Bonaparte

WHERE THERE IS RUIN,
THERE IS HOPE
FOR TREASURE.

Rumi

BECOME THE
PERSON YOU'VE
ALWAYS WANTED
TO BE

NOT ONLY STRIKE
WHILE THE IRON IS
HOT, BUT MAKE IT HOT
BY STRIKING.

Oliver Cromwell

NO ONE REALLY KNOWS
WHY THEY ARE ALIVE
UNTIL THEY KNOW WHAT
THEY'D DIE FOR.

Martin Luther King Jr

MAKE EVERY
DAY COUNT

A MAN IS NOT FINISHED
WHEN HE IS DEFEATED.
HE IS FINISHED WHEN
HE QUITS.

Richard Nixon

THE GREATEST GLORY
IN LIVING LIES NOT IN
NEVER FALLING, BUT IN
RISING EVERY TIME
WE FALL.

Nelson Mandela

SHARE YOUR GIFT WITH THE WORLD

WHEREVER YOU GO, GO WITH ALL YOUR HEART.

Confucius

WHATEVER THE
MIND OF MAN CAN
CONCEIVE AND BELIEVE,
IT CAN ACHIEVE.

Napoleon Hill

WITHOUT
OBSTACLES, LIFE
WOULD JUST BE A
RACE – AND THAT
WOULDN'T BE HALF
AS MUCH FUN

WELL DONE IS BETTER
THAN WELL SAID.

Benjamin Franklin

ONE WHO CONTINUES TO ADVANCE WILL WIN IN THE END.

Daisaku Ikeda

HAVE NO
REGRETS

YOU CAN'T START THE NEXT CHAPTER OF YOUR LIFE IF YOU KEEP RE-READING THE LAST ONE.

Anonymous

I DO NOT BELIEVE
IN TAKING THE RIGHT
DECISION, I TAKE
A DECISION AND
MAKE IT RIGHT.

Muhammad Ali

FOLLOW YOUR
OWN PATH

I DREAM THINGS THAT NEVER WERE; AND I SAY, 'WHY NOT?'

George Bernard Shaw

WRITE IT. SHOOT IT.
PUBLISH IT. CROCHET IT,
SAUTÉ IT, WHATEVER.
MAKE.

Joss Whedon

STAND TALL
AND MAKE SURE
YOU'RE HEARD

WE ARE ALL WORMS,
BUT I DO BELIEVE THAT
I AM A GLOW-WORM.

Winston Churchill

THE GREATEST
DISCOVERY OF ANY
GENERATION IS THAT A
HUMAN CAN ALTER HIS
LIFE BY ALTERING
HIS ATTITUDE.

William James

BE THE BEST
POSSIBLE
VERSION OF
YOURSELF

EVERYTHING THAT IS
DONE IN THE WORLD IS
DONE BY HOPE.

Martin Luther King Jr

SOMETIMES, AS WE'RE
STUMBLING ALONG
IN THE DARK, WE HIT
SOMETHING GOOD.

Susan Ee

ENJOY THE
STORIES THAT
UNFOLD IN THE
REAL WORLD —
NOT THE ONES
ON THE TV

WITH OUR THOUGHTS WE MAKE THE WORLD.

Buddha

YOU HAVE TO TEACH YOUR
HEART AND MIND HOW TO
SING TOGETHER... THEN
YOU'LL HEAR THE SOUND
OF YOUR SOUL.

Renée Carlino

WHATEVER IT IS, MAKE IT HAPPEN!

IT DOESN'T MATTER
WHAT WE ARE. IT
MATTERS WHAT WE DO.

Michelle Hodkin

AS ONE GOES THROUGH LIFE, ONE LEARNS THAT IF YOU DON'T PADDLE YOUR OWN CANOE, YOU DON'T MOVE.

Katharine Hepburn

DOORS ARE MADE
TO BE OPENED;
LOCKS ARE MADE
TO FIT A KEY

LIFE KEEPS THROWING ME LEMONS BECAUSE I MAKE THE BEST LEMONADE.

King James Gadsden

IF YOU DON'T LIKE
SOMETHING, CHANGE IT;
IF YOU CAN'T CHANGE IT,
CHANGE THE WAY YOU
THINK ABOUT IT.

Mary Engelbreit

EVERY DAWN IS A
NEW BEGINNING,
A TIME TO START
A NEW STORY

THE MOST POWERFUL
RELATIONSHIP YOU
WILL EVER HAVE IS THE
RELATIONSHIP WITH
YOURSELF.

Steve Maraboli

THE GREATEST
PLEASURE IN LIFE IS
DOING WHAT PEOPLE SAY
YOU CANNOT DO.

Walter Bagehot

LOVE YOURSELF

FAITH IS THE BIRD THAT
FEELS THE LIGHT AND
SINGS WHEN THE DAWN
IS STILL DARK.

Rabindranath Tagore

LOOK UP TO THE SKY.
YOU'LL NEVER FIND
RAINBOWS IF YOU'RE
LOOKING DOWN.

Charlie Chaplin

BE FOOTLOOSE
AND FANCY-FREE!

BELIEVE THAT LIFE IS
WORTH LIVING, AND
YOUR BELIEF WILL HELP
CREATE THE FACT.

William James

THERE ARE NO
TRAFFIC JAMS ALONG
THE EXTRA MILE.

Roger Staubach

YOU CAN DO IT.
ALL YOU HAVE
TO DO IS TRY

I AVOID LOOKING
FORWARD OR BACKWARD,
AND TRY TO KEEP
LOOKING UPWARD.

Charlotte Brontë

YOU MUST EXPECT
GREAT THINGS OF
YOURSELF BEFORE YOU
CAN DO THEM.

Michael Jordan

YOU ONLY
LIVE ONCE

NOBODY MADE A
GREATER MISTAKE THAN
HE WHO DID NOTHING
BECAUSE HE COULD ONLY
DO A LITTLE.

Edmund Burke

IT'S MORE FUN TO THINK
OF THE FUTURE THAN
DWELL ON THE PAST.

Sara Shepard

LOOK AT LIFE
FROM A NEW
ANGLE TODAY

AMAZING HOW WE CAN LIGHT TOMORROW WITH TODAY.

Elizabeth Barrett Browning

WE CAN DO ANYTHING WE
WANT TO DO IF WE STICK
TO IT LONG ENOUGH.

Helen Keller

WHEN'S THE BEST TIME TO START? NOW!

YOUR GREATEST SELF
HAS BEEN WAITING
YOUR WHOLE LIFE;
DON'T MAKE IT WAIT
ANY LONGER.

Steve Maraboli

AIM FOR THE MOON.
IF YOU MISS, YOU MAY
HIT A STAR.

W. Clement Stone

DRESS TO
IMPRESS

WHAT YOU DO TODAY CAN IMPROVE ALL YOUR TOMORROWS.

Ralph Marston

THERE IS ALWAYS ROOM
AT THE TOP.

Daniel Webster

TALK TO
SOMEONE NEW.
YOU COULD MAKE
THEIR DAY — AND
THEY MIGHT
MAKE YOURS

MARCH ON, AND FEAR
NOT THE THORNS, OR
THE SHARP STONES ON
LIFE'S PATH.

Kahlil Gibran

OPPORTUNITY DOES NOT
KNOCK. IT PRESENTS
ITSELF WHEN YOU BEAT
DOWN THE DOOR.

Kyle Chandler

DON'T RACE
FOR THE FINISH
LINE — ENJOY
THE JOURNEY

MY SUN SETS TO
RISE AGAIN.

Robert Browning

I AM NOT AFRAID OF
STORMS, FOR I AM
LEARNING HOW TO
SAIL MY SHIP.

Louisa May Alcott

TURN YOUR
DREAMS INTO
REALITY

FOLLOW YOUR DREAMS, WORK HARD, PRACTISE AND PERSEVERE.

Sasha Cohen

AS SOON AS YOU START
TO PURSUE A DREAM,
YOUR LIFE WAKES UP
AND EVERYTHING
HAS MEANING.

Barbara Sher

Meet Esme!

Our feathered friend Esme loves finding perfect quotes for the perfect occasion, and is almost as good at collecting them as she is at collecting twigs for her nest. She's always full of joy and happiness, singing her messages of goodwill in this series of uplifting, heart-warming books.

Follow Esme on Twitter at **@EsmeTheBird**.

For more information about our books, find us on Facebook at **Summersdale Publishers** and follow us on Twitter at **@Summersdale**.

www.summersdale.com

SEIZE THE DAY!